18153096 1

HUMAN BODY

By
Emilie Dufresne

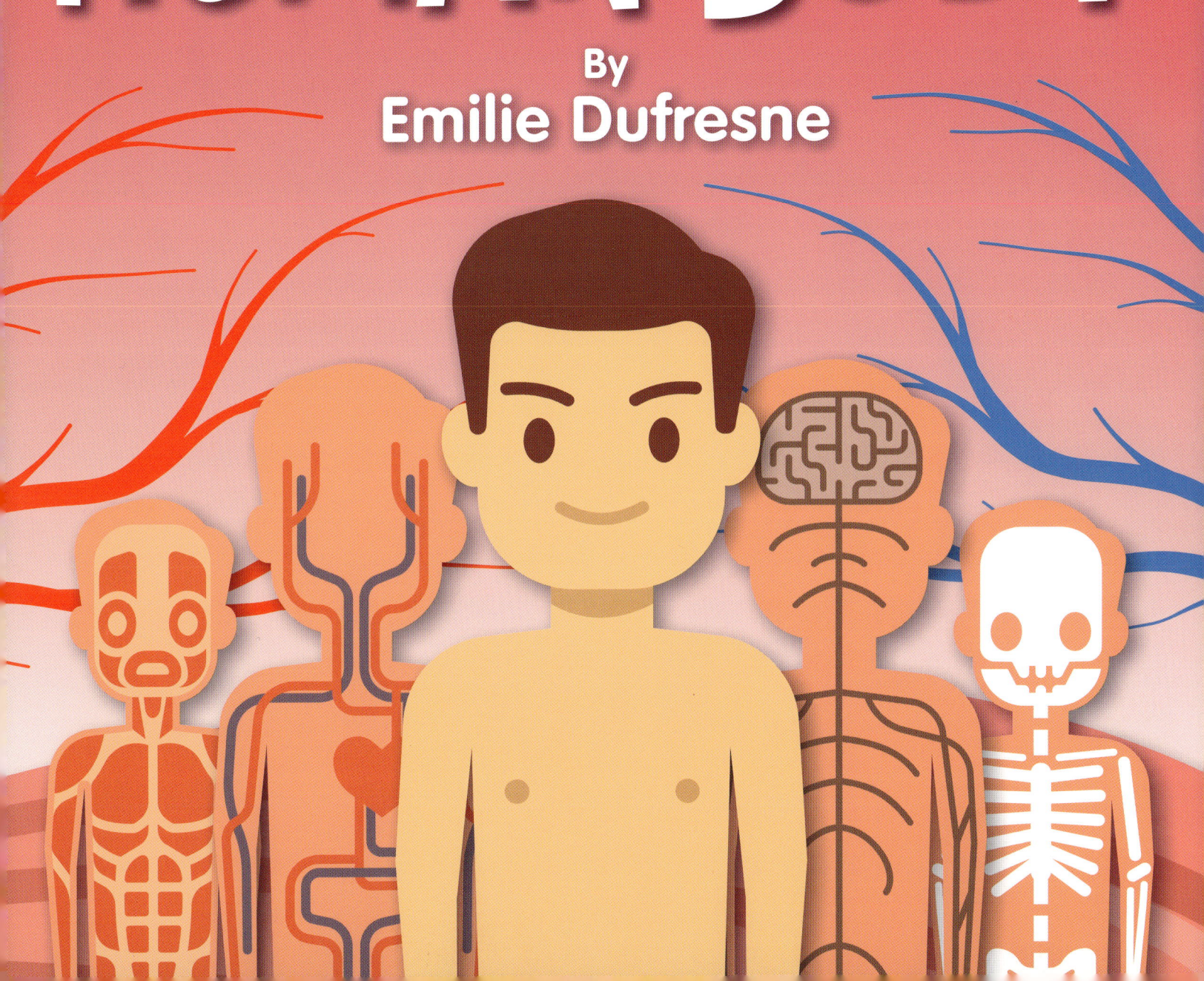

BookLife
PUBLISHING

©2019
BookLife Publishing Ltd.
King's Lynn
Norfolk PE30 4LS
All rights reserved.
Printed in Malaysia.

A catalogue record for this
book is available from the
British Library.

ISBN: 978-1-78637-853-8

Written by:
Emilie Dufresne

Edited by:
Madeline Tyler

Designed by:
Gareth Liddington

Photocredits:

4 - ann131313. ONYXpr, 5 - Amaro_K, aliaksei kruhlenia, Anna Frajtova, 6 - aliaksei kruhlenia, HappyPictures, Stocklifemax, 7 - Iconic Bestiary, Vsevolod Shaposhnikov, Makc, 8 - Chalintra,B, 11 - nur fatoni, Laia Design Lab, Ser_bia, BlueRingMedia, Volha Shaukavets, 12 - Sudowoodo, 13 - MicroOne, DarkestBlue, Glinskaja Olga, 14 - Panda Vector, 15 - Panimoni, 16 - elenabsl, 18 - Nataliya Dolotko, Rvector, 19 - AlZhi, Lucia Fox, 20 - Olesya Kuznetsova, Vasylyna Halun, 21 - Julia Tim, Sharlaev Maksim, 22 - Aksanaku, 23 - ankomando.

Images are courtesy of Shutterstock.com. With thanks to Getty Images, Thinkstock Photo and iStockphoto.

All facts, statistics, web addresses and URLs in this book were verified as valid and accurate at time of writing. No responsibility for any changes to external websites or references can be accepted by either the author or publisher.

CONTENTS

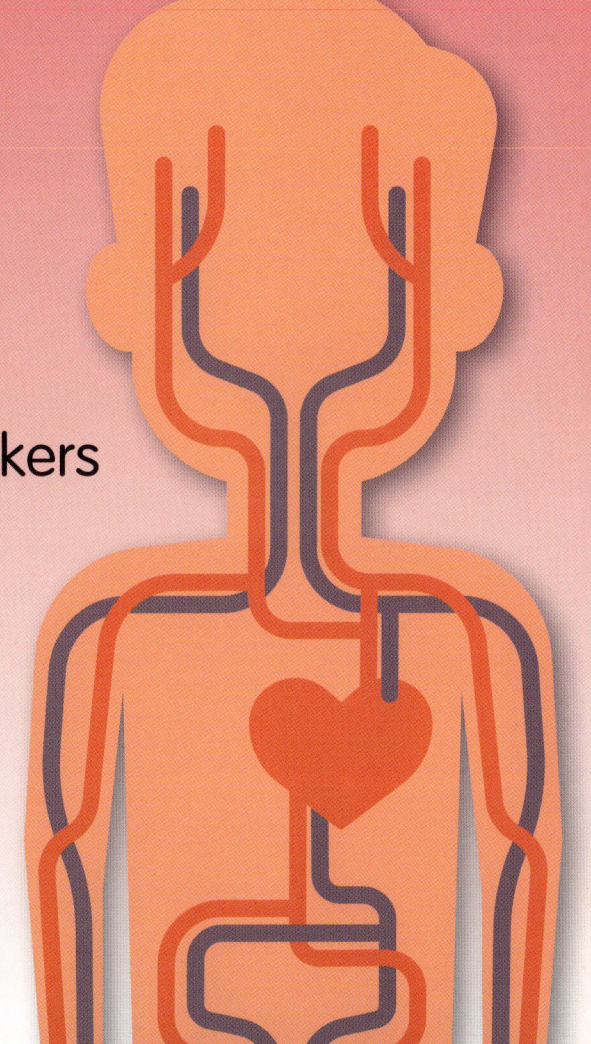

THE HUMAN BODY

The human body is made up of lots of different parts that all have different jobs. They all work together to keep you alive.

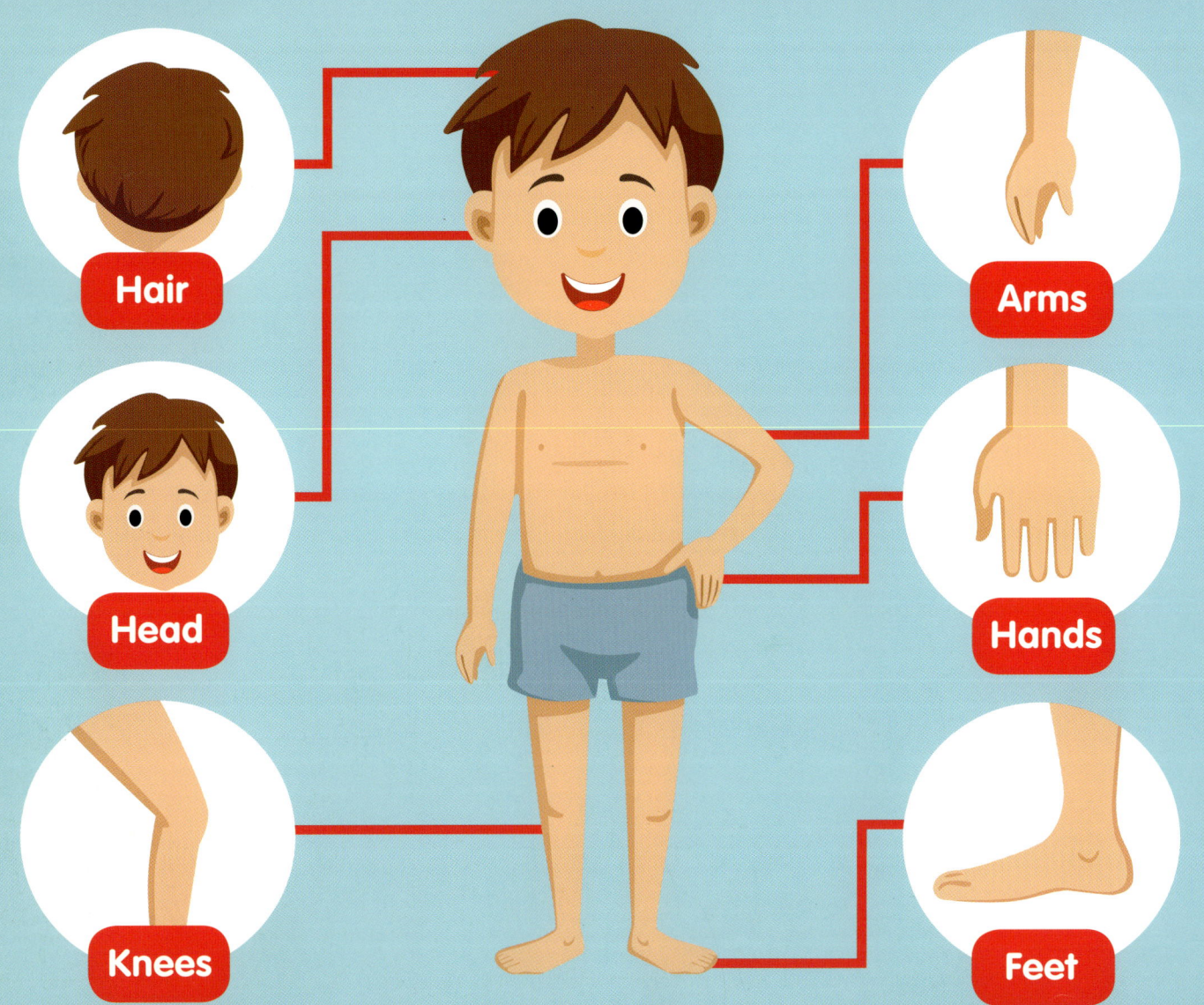

Hair

Head

Knees

Arms

Hands

Feet

Human bodies need a few simple things to stay alive and healthy. These things are:

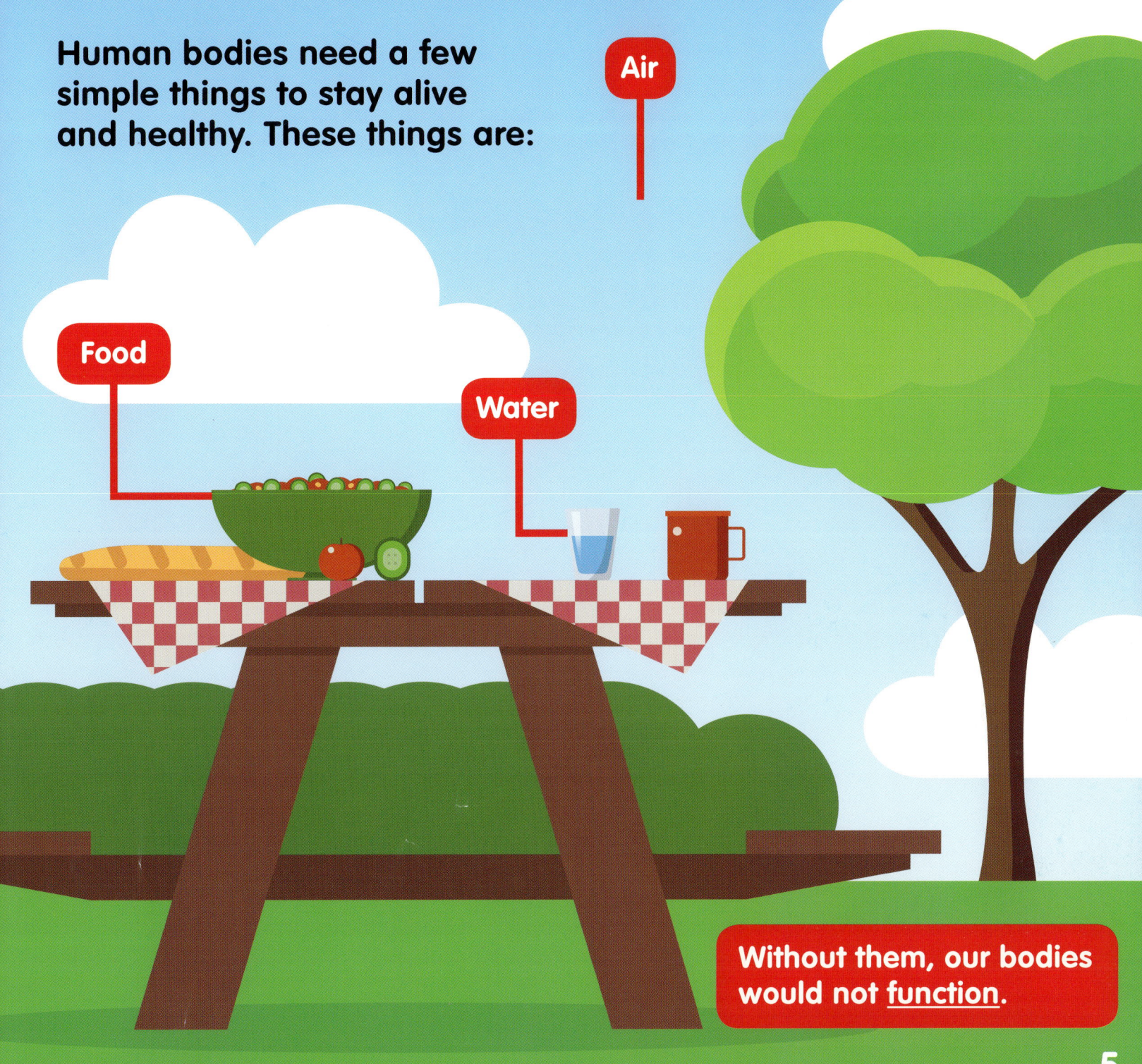

Air

Food

Water

Without them, our bodies would not <u>function</u>.

THE SKELETON

The skeleton is like the frame of the body. It is the part that holds you upright. Without your skeleton, you would be like a tent without poles.

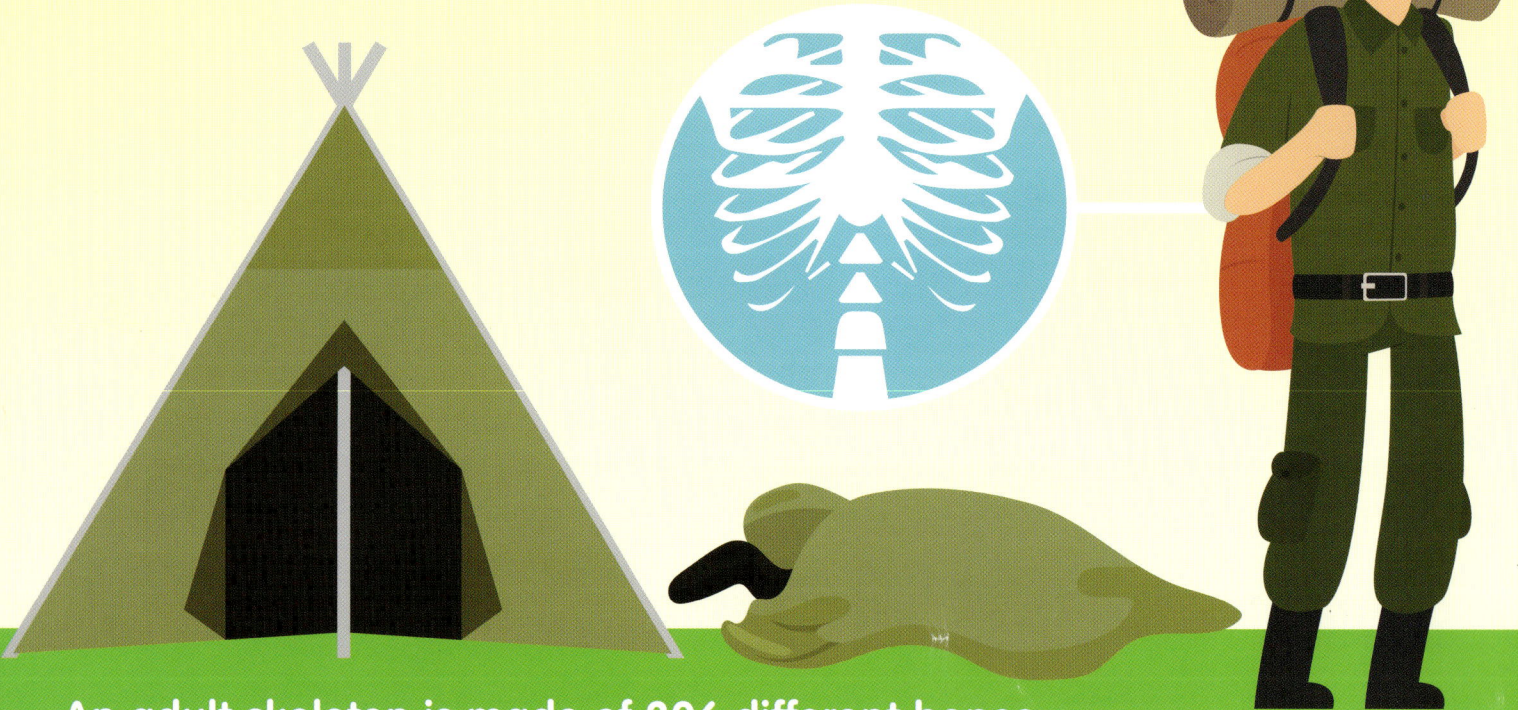

An adult skeleton is made of 206 different bones.

It is important to have strong and healthy bones. To grow strong bones, you will need these three things:

Vitamin D

Exercise

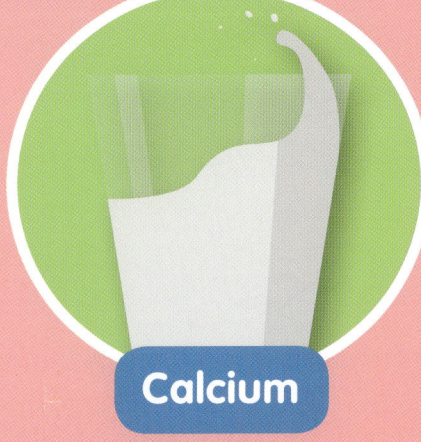

Calcium

Your bones will continue to grow until you are around 20 years old.

THE SENSES

Humans have five main senses that help us take in the world around us. These are: taste, touch, hearing, sight and smell.

TASTE

The tongue helps us taste. There are five main tastes. These are: bitter, sour, salty, sweet and <u>umami</u>.

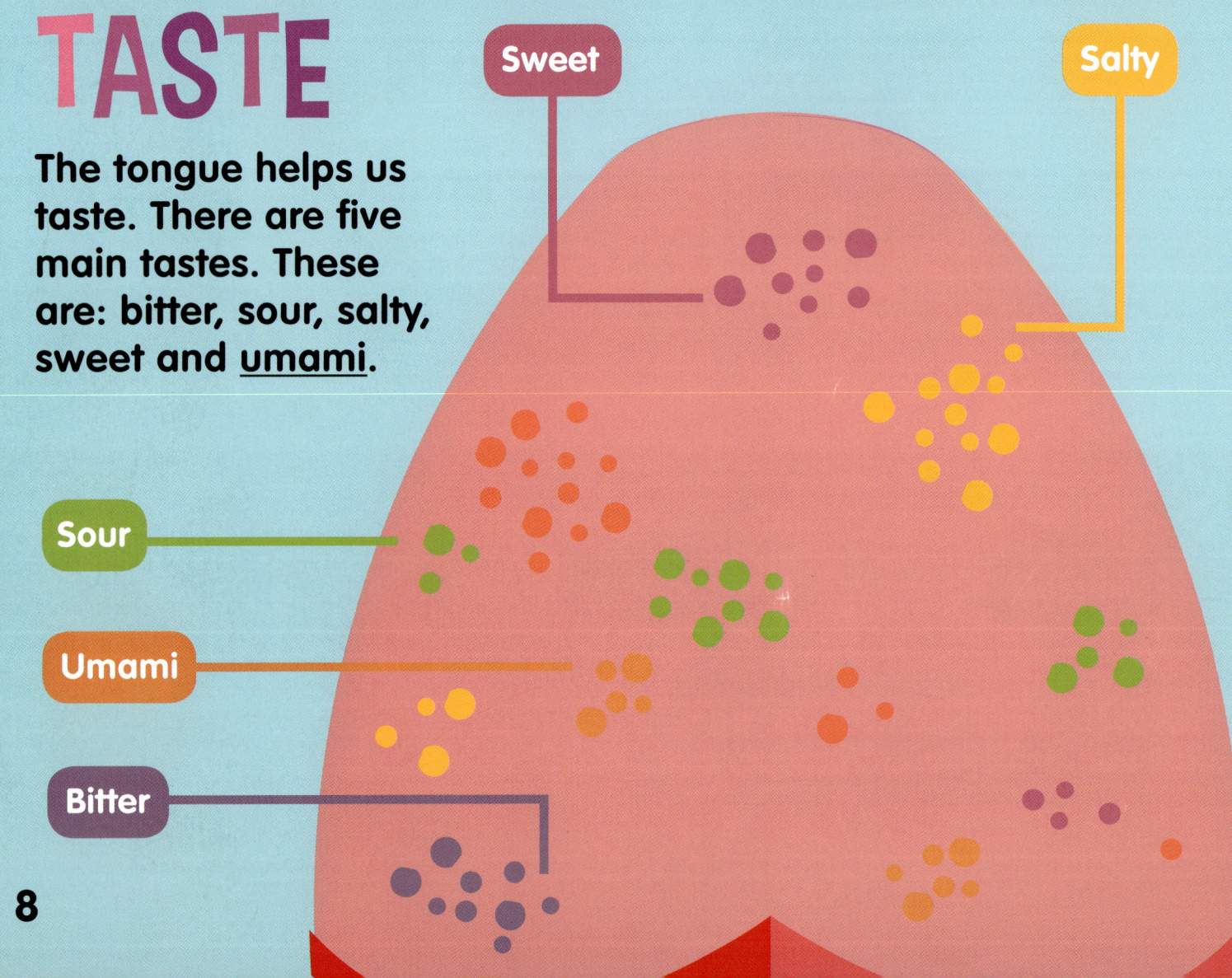

Sweet

Salty

Sour

Umami

Bitter

TOUCH

Our skin is very sensitive and can help us feel the world around us. Here are some of the things we can feel when we touch things.

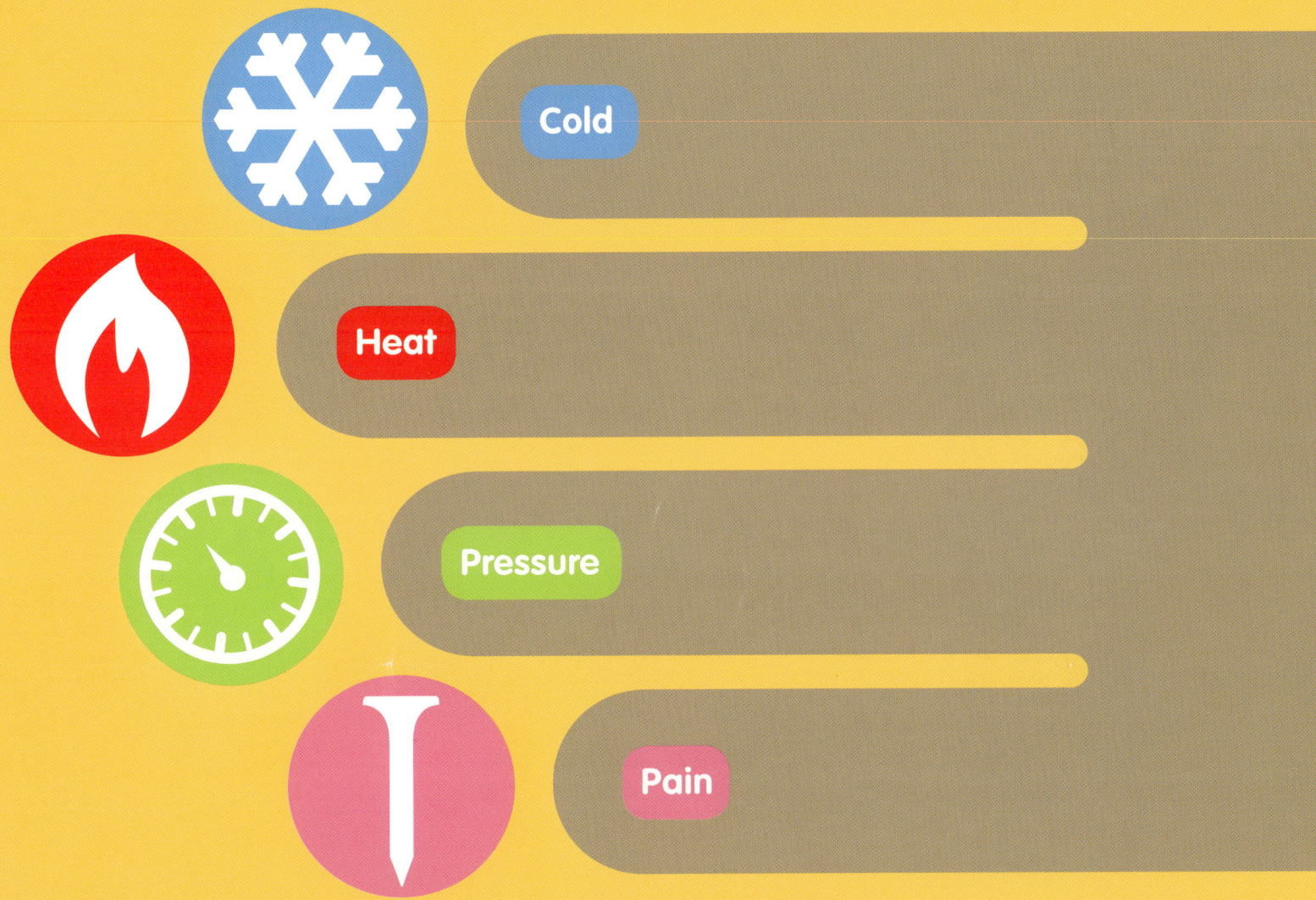

Cold

Heat

Pressure

Pain

HEARING

Sound travels into our ears. This is how we hear what is happening around us.

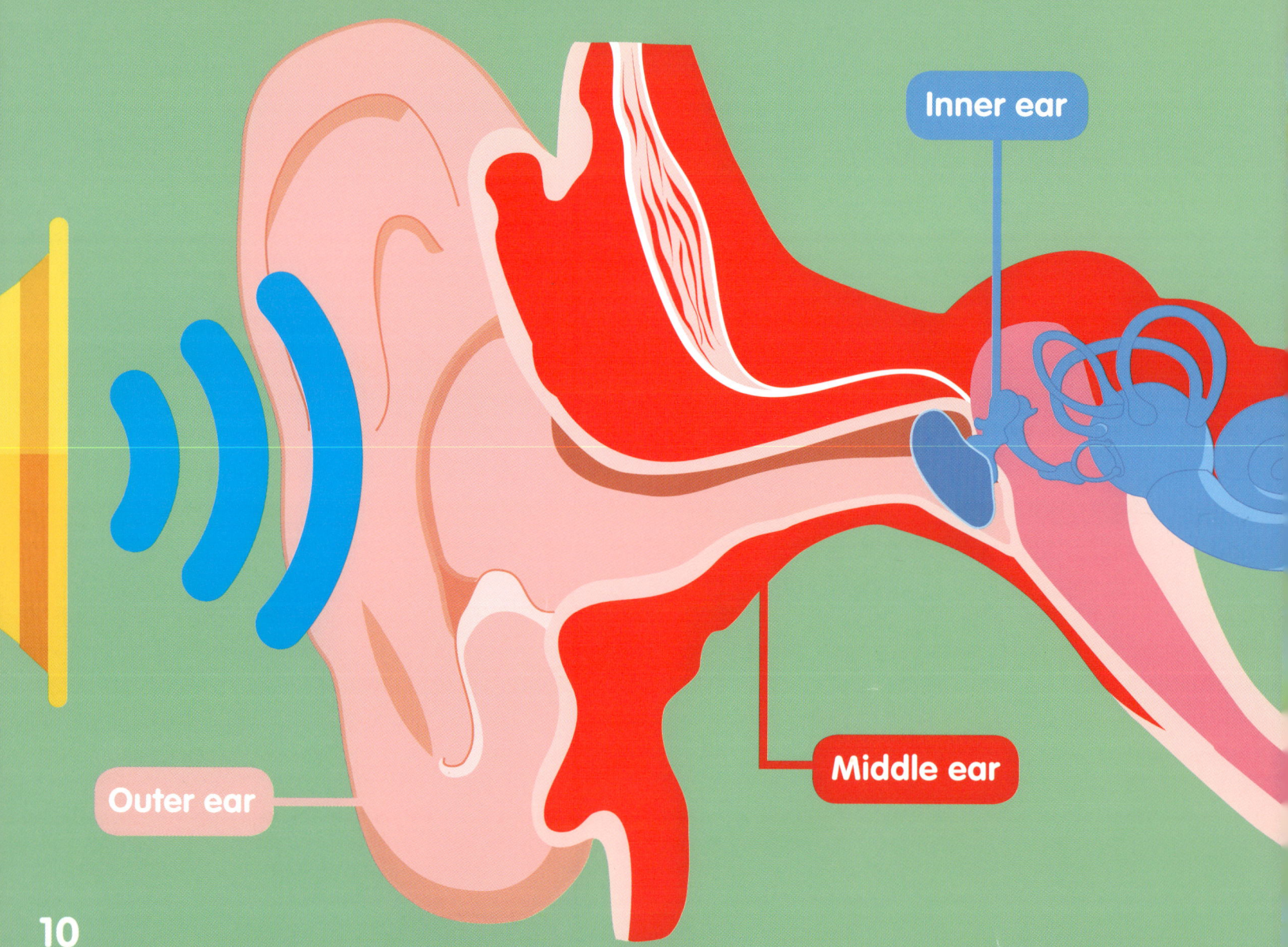

Inner ear

Middle ear

Outer ear

SIGHT

Our eyes let us see things. The pupil in the middle of the eye gets bigger in low light to help us see, and smaller in bright light to protect our eyes.

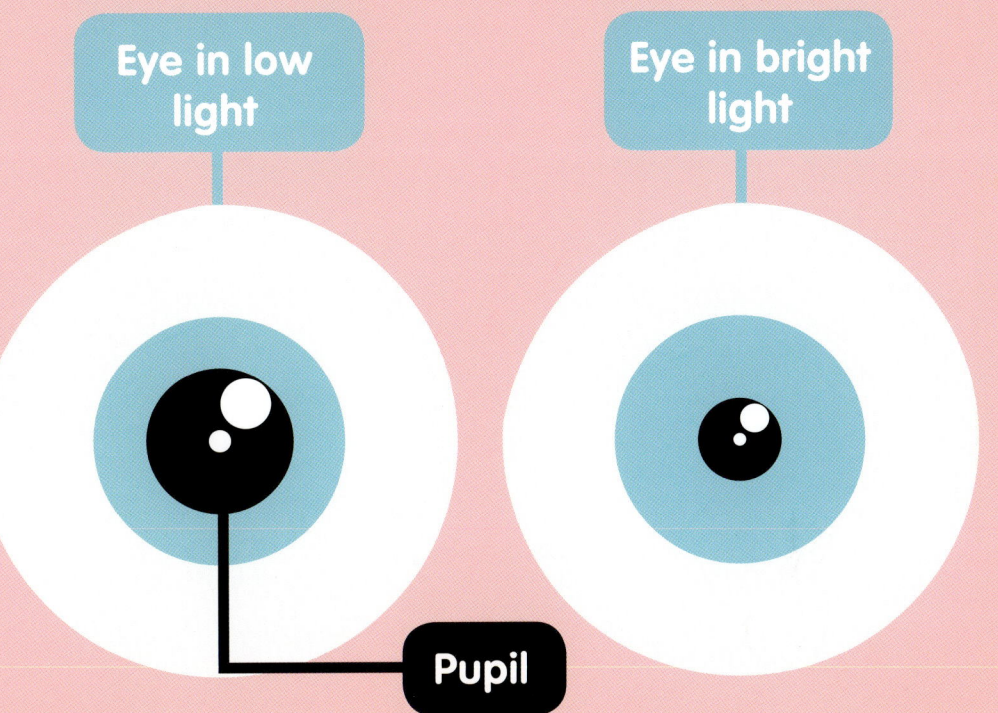

Eye in low light

Eye in bright light

Pupil

SMELL

Noses help us smell things. Smelling food can help us know when something might be tasty or when something might not be good to eat anymore.

11

THE MUSCLES

Muscles are parts of the body that help us to move.

The human body has more than 600 muscles.

Muscles

Muscles often work in pairs. One will contract (get tighter) while the other relaxes (gets looser).

Contracted

Relaxed

Relaxed

Contracted

Some muscles work without us having to think about them. For example, your heart is a muscle that pumps blood around your body, even when you're sleeping.

We have to make some other muscles in our bodies move, such as the ones in our arms and legs.

Heart

PUMPING BLOOD

Your heart is located slightly to the left of the centre of your chest and is around the size of your fist.

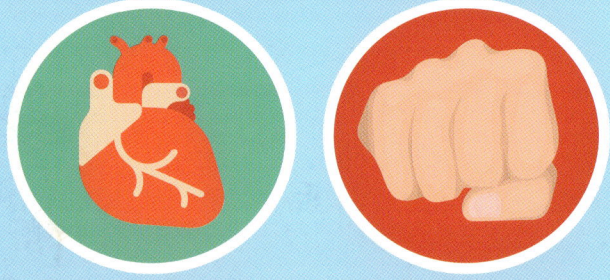

Most people have around five litres of blood in their body at any one time.

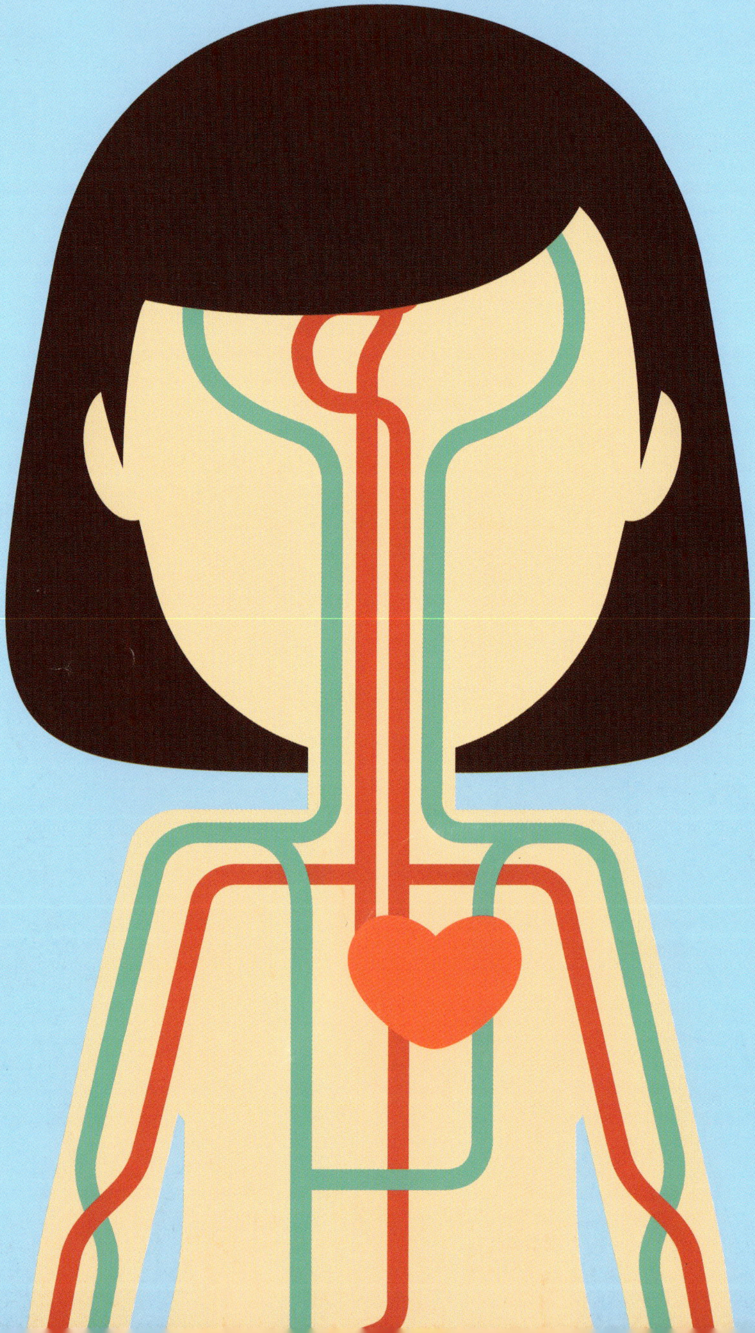

A person's heart usually pumps around 80 times every minute, but your heart rate might be anything between 60 and 100 beats per minute.

60
SECONDS

BREATHING

We breathe using our mouth, nose and lungs. This is how we get oxygen into our body. Oxygen is a <u>gas</u> that humans need in order to stay alive.

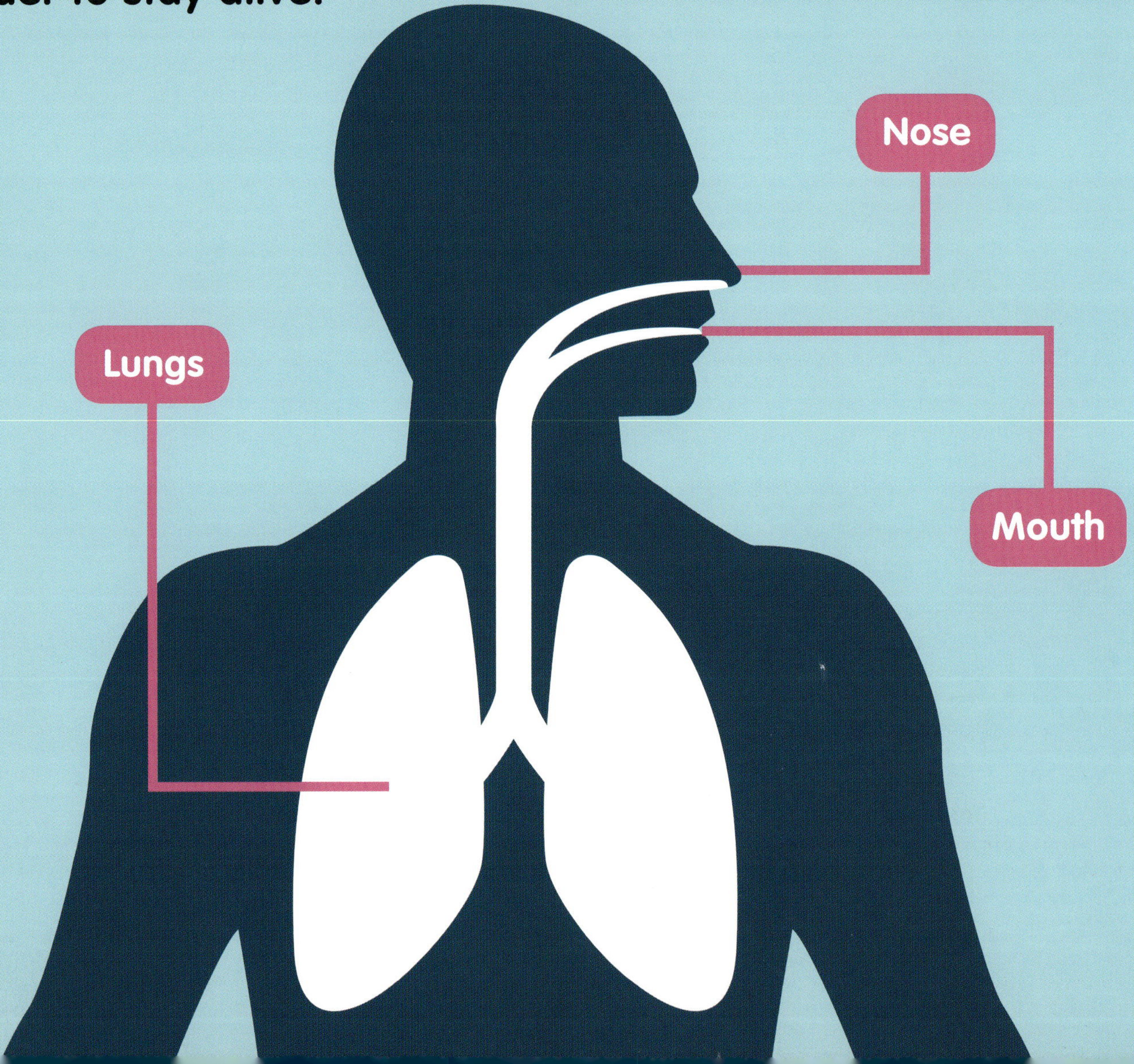

Nose

Lungs

Mouth

As a person gets older, their breathing rate changes. Older people need fewer breaths per minute than younger people.

Adult

Ten years old

Three years old

Newborn

30–60 breaths per minute

25–35 breaths per minute

20–30 breaths per minute

14–18 breaths per minute

17

PROTECTING YOUR BODY

Our bodies are always trying to stop us from getting ill. Here are some of the ways our bodies help us to stay well.

We get <u>immunity</u> to some illnesses from our mothers. They pass on their immunity to us in the <u>womb</u> and through their milk.

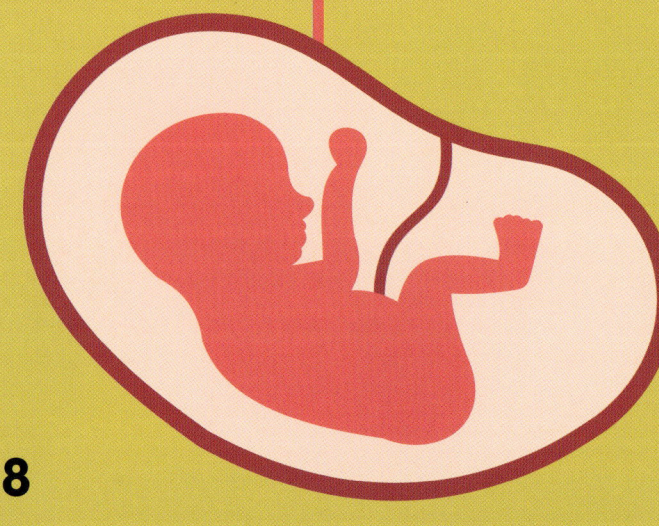

Our skin provides a barrier to the world.

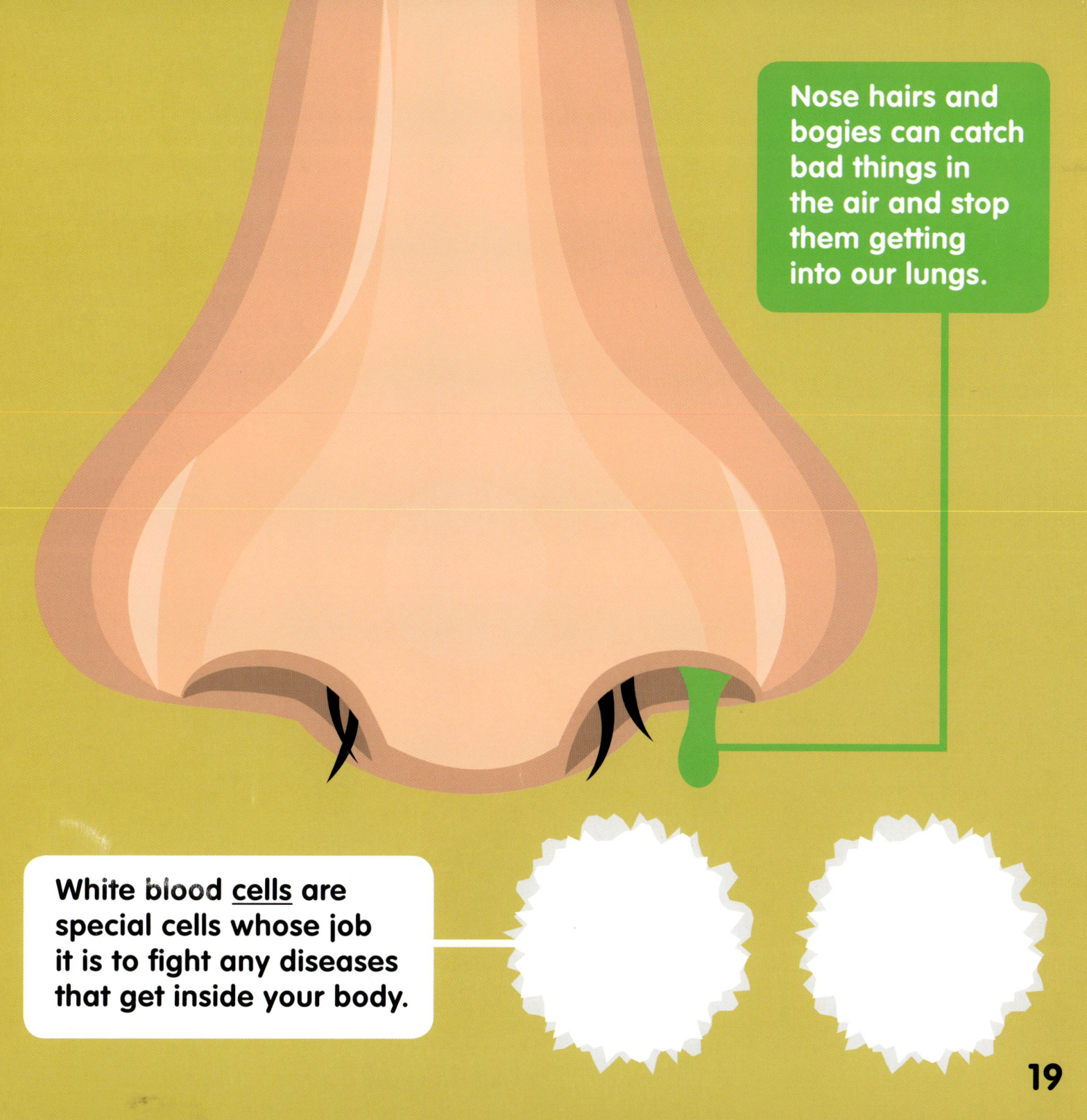

Nose hairs and bogies can catch bad things in the air and stop them getting into our lungs.

White blood <u>cells</u> are special cells whose job it is to fight any diseases that get inside your body.

19

HEALTHY LIVING

It's important to eat a balanced diet to keep your body healthy. This means eating the right amounts of certain foods.

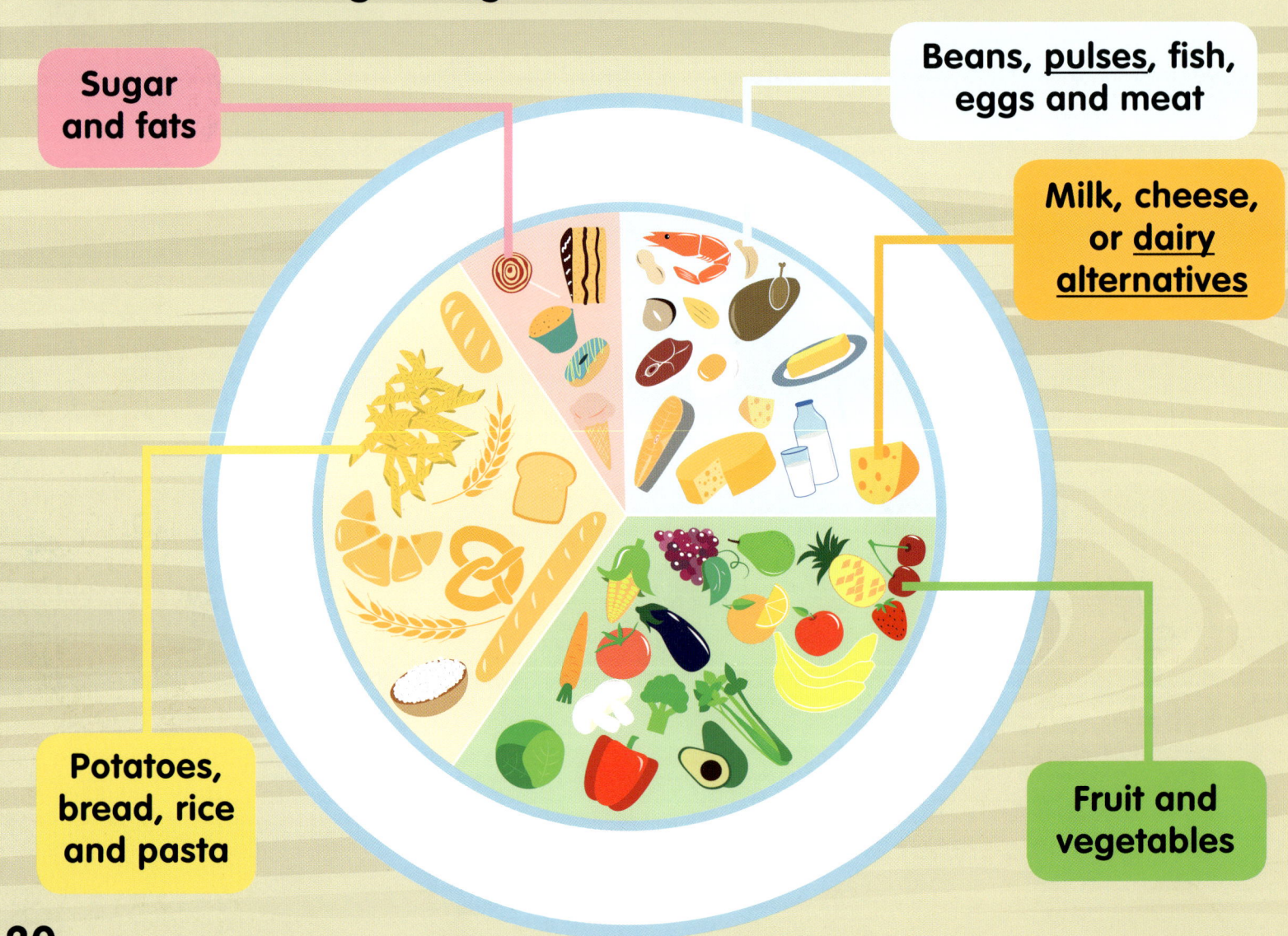

Sugar and fats

Beans, _pulses_, fish, eggs and meat

Milk, cheese, or _dairy alternatives_

Potatoes, bread, rice and pasta

Fruit and vegetables

Your body needs water in order to work properly. Children aged between five and eight should drink around one litre of water every day. This is around five glasses.

You should also try to exercise for 60 minutes each day. This can be climbing, playing or swimming.

HUMAN BODY RECORD BREAKERS

The largest feet ever recorded were 47 centimetres long.

The world record for the longest human tongue is just over 10 centimetres.

The longest head hair ever recorded is over five and a half metres long.

The world record for hula hooping without stopping is 74 hours and 54 minutes. How long can you hula hoop for?

23

GLOSSARY

cells	the basic building blocks that make up all living things
dairy alternatives	products that taste like dairy but are not made from animal products
function	work properly
gas	a thing that is like air, which spreads out to fill any space available
half	one of two equal parts of something
immunity	having protection from a disease or illness
pulses	the edible seeds of certain plants such as peas, beans and lentils
umami	one of the five basic tastes – foods that have a strong umami taste include soy sauce, mushrooms and tomatoes
womb	the fluid-filled sac that some babies grow in

INDEX

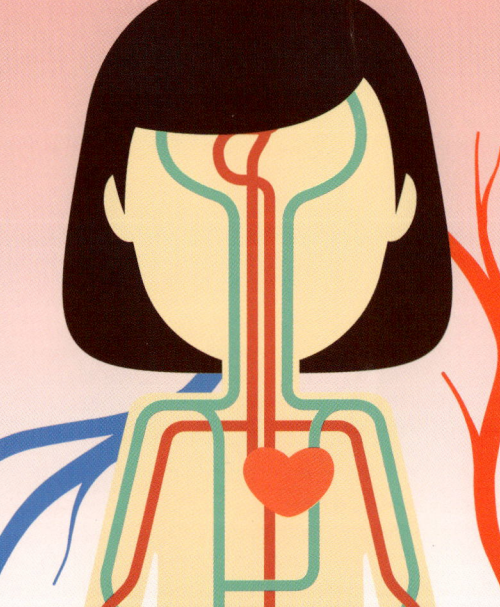